SIGHT READING
and
EAR TRAINING

E. L. Lancaster and
Gayle Kowalchyk
with David Carr Glover

© 1988 BELWIN-MILLS PUBLISHING CORP.
All Rights Administered by WARNER BROS. PUBLICATIONS U.S. INC.
All Rights Reserved including Public Performance for Profit

Design and Illustration: Jeannette Aquino

FOREWORD

Teacher and Parents:

Sight reading and ear training are two of the most important skills for any musician. Consequently, they should be developed systematically with performance, technical and theory skills from the time that keyboard study begins.

SIGHT READING AND EAR TRAINING, Primer Level, correlates with **LESSONS**, Primer Level. As new concepts are introduced in the lessons book, they are reinforced visually and aurally in the sight reading and ear training book. SIGHT READING AND EAR TRAINING can be used with equal success in private and group lessons.

The reading exercises in this series are based on the premise that students develop secure reading skills by first playing in specific patterns and gradually moving out of these patterns. The recognition of intervals is crucial to the development of good reading habits. In addition, students must be able to quickly identify individual notes and patterns (melodic, harmonic and rhythmic). Students should practice the assigned reading pages daily and complete any written work on the pages prior to the lesson. At the lesson, the teacher should hear each example.

Note flashes and *interval flashes* are designed to be used like flashcards. They may be shown rapidly to the student and then covered or taken away to aid with the memory process. All of the examples are designed to aid the student in recognizing familiar concepts and executing them at the keyboard.

Listening pages reinforce the concepts being studied from an aural standpoint. They should be completed in the lesson or may be done at home if a parent is able to play the musical examples. It may be necessary to repeat the ear training examples several times for some students. Rhythmic examples that are not notated on the staff should be clapped.

The Teacher's Pages (38-48) contain examples and answers for all of the exercises in the book.

Supplementary materials correlated with
LESSONS, Primer Level, from the
David Carr Glover METHOD for PIANO

SIGHT READING AND EAR TRAINING .... Introduce with Page 6
THEORY .... Page 8
TECHNIC .... Page 11
PERFORMANCE .... Page 13

Additional teaching aids include
Music Assignment Book, Glover Music Magic Slate,
Music Flash Cards, Manuscript Writing Book.

Contents

		Page
Listening	- High, Middle, Low	4
Listening	- Quarter and Half Notes	5
Pre-Reading	- Two and Three Black Keys	6
Listening	- Whole Note	7
Listening	- Up-Down, ♩ , ♪ and o Notes	8
Pre-Reading	- Middle C Position	9
Listening	- Steps, Skips, Repeats	10
Listening	- Steps, Skips, Repeats	11
Listening	- 2nds and 3rds	12
Reading	- 2nds and 3rds	13
Listening	- Steps and Skips, 2nds and 3rds	14
Reading	- 2nds and 3rds	15
Listening	- Quarter Rest, 2nds and 3rds	16
Reading	- New C Position	17
Listening	- Steps and Skips	18
Listening	- Legato, 2nds and 3rds	19
Reading	- C Position, Tie	20
Listening	- Tie	21
Listening	- Melodic and Harmonic Intervals	22
Reading	- Interval of a 4th	23
Listening	- Interval of a 4th	24
Reading	- Interval of a 5th	25
Listening	- Interval of a 5th	26
Listening	- Flat Sign	27
Reading	- Flat Sign	28
Listening	- Sharp Sign	29
Reading	- Sharp Sign	30
Reading	- G Position, Staccato	31
Listening	- G Position, Staccato	32
Reading	- Review (99-100)	33
Listening	- Review (101-103)	34
Listening	- Review (104-115)	35
Listening	- Review (116-118)	36
Reading	- Review (119-122)	37
	Teacher's Pages	38-48

Listening
HIGH, MIDDLE, LOW

1. Listen to notes that make high, middle or low sounds.
   Circle the correct answer.

   a. high   b. high   c. high

       middle   middle   middle

       low   low   low

2. Listen to two notes. Is the second note higher or lower?
   Circle the correct answer.

   a. higher   b. higher   c. higher

       lower   lower   lower

3. Do you hear one note or more than one note?
   Circle the correct answer.

   a. one   b. one   c. one

       more   more   more

4. Is the longer note played first or second?
   Circle the correct answer.

   a. first   b. first   c. first

       second   second   second

Use with pages 6-7, LESSONS, Primer Level.

Listening
QUARTER AND HALF NOTES

5. Circle the rhythm pattern that you hear.

   a.    b.    c.

6. Listen to two rhythm patterns. Are they the same or different? Circle the correct answer.

   a. same   b. same   c. same

   different   different   different

7. Do the sounds go up, down or stay the same? Circle the correct answer.

   a. up   b. up   c. up

   down   down   down

   same   same   same

8. Look and listen to the rhythm pattern. Draw the missing note (♩ or 𝅗𝅥) under the arrow.

9. You will hear one of the following rhythm patterns: ♩ ♩ 𝅗𝅥 or 𝅗𝅥 𝅗𝅥 or ♩ ♩ ♩ ♩ . Draw the one you hear.

   a.   b.   c.

Use with pages 6-7, LESSONS, Primer Level.

Pre-Reading
TWO AND THREE BLACK KEYS

10. *FLASHES USING TWO BLACK KEYS: Play and count aloud the examples using the given position.

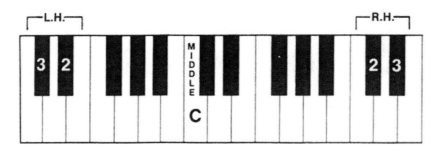

a. Left hand

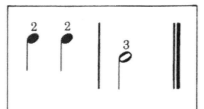

b. Right hand

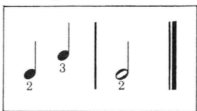

11. *FLASHES USING THREE BLACK KEYS: Play and count aloud the examples using the given position.

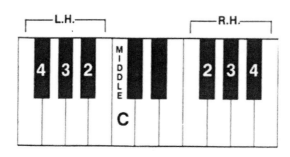

a. Left hand

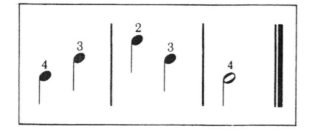

b. Right hand

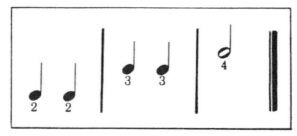

*See Foreword for an explanation of flashes.

Use with pages 6-7, LESSONS, Primer Level.

Listening
WHOLE NOTE

12. Circle the rhythm pattern that you hear.

13. Listen to two rhythm patterns. Are they the same or different? Circle the correct answer.

    a. same   b. same   c. same

    different   different   different

14. Read the words to "Bedtime" and complete the notes to form the correct rhythm. Use ♩ 𝅗𝅥 and 𝅝

BEDTIME

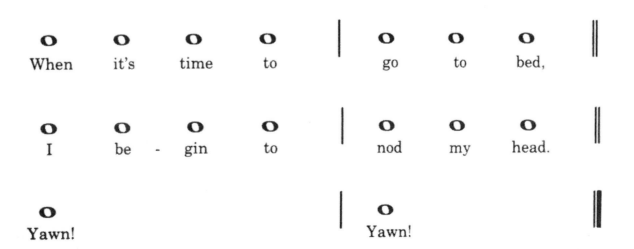

Use with pages 6-7, LESSONS, Primer Level.

Listening

UP-DOWN, ♩ , ♩ AND o NOTES

15. Listen to the music alphabet. Draw an arrow in the direction that it is moving and label up or down.

    Examples:

    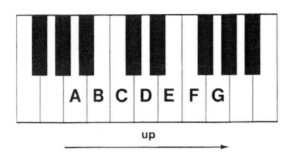

    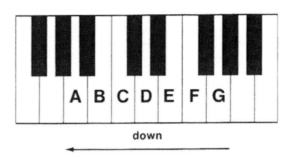

    a.   b.

    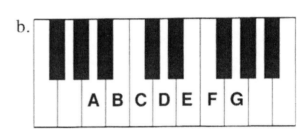

16. Look and listen to the rhythm pattern. Draw the missing note (♩ ♩ or o) under the arrow.

    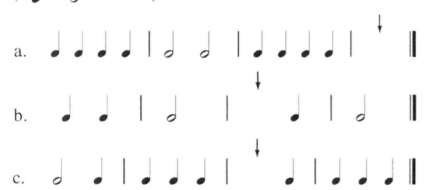

17. Listen to four notes that move up or down the keyboard by steps. The starting key is shown. Write the letter names on the keyboard of the notes that you hear.

    a.   b.

    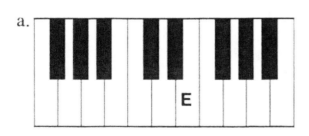

    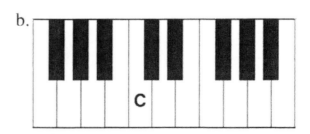

Use with pages 7-8, LESSONS, Primer Level.

Pre-Reading
MIDDLE C POSITION

18. FLASHES USING MIDDLE C POSITION: Play and count aloud the examples using the middle C position.

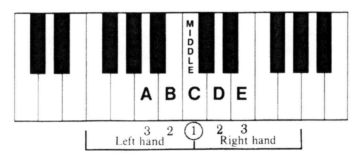

a. Left hand

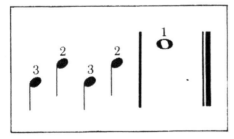

b. Right hand

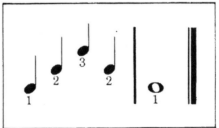

c. Left hand

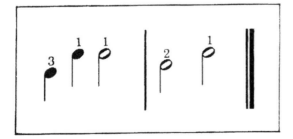

d. Right hand

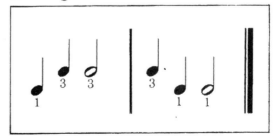

Use with pages 9-11, LESSONS, Primer Level.

Listening
STEPS, SKIPS, REPEATS

19. Listen to two notes. The second note will step up or step down from the first note. The starting key is shown. Write the letter name on the keyboard of the second note that you hear.

a.

b.

c.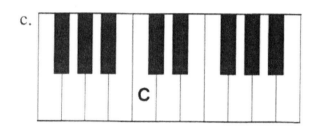

d.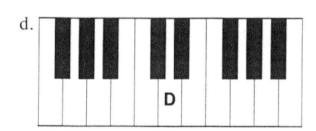

20. Listen to two notes. The second note will skip up or skip down from the first note. The starting key is shown. Write the letter name on the keyboard of the second note that you hear.

a.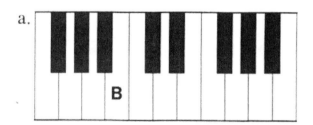

b.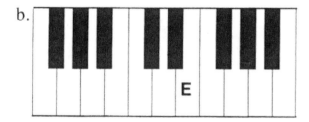

c.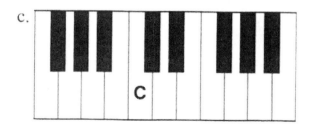

d.

Use with pages 9-11, LESSONS, Primer Level.

Listening
STEPS, SKIPS, REPEATS

21. Listen to two notes. Is the second note a step or a repeat?
    Circle the correct answer.

    a. step   b. step   c. step

        repeat   repeat   repeat

22. Listen to two notes. Is the second note a skip or a repeat?
    Circle the correct answer.

    a. skip   b. skip   c. skip

        repeat   repeat   repeat

23. Listen to two notes. Is the second note a step or a skip?
    Circle the correct answer.

    a. step   b. step   c. step

        skip   skip   skip

Use with pages 9-11, LESSONS, Primer Level.

Listening
2NDS AND 3RDS

24. Listen to intervals of a 2nd or 3rd. Circle the correct answer.

25. Listen to each rhythm pattern. Add the correct dynamic marking (f or p) on the line in front of each example.

26. Read the words to "Teddy Bear" and complete the notes to form the correct rhythm. Use ♩ and 𝅗𝅥

TEDDY BEAR

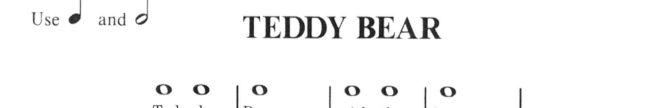

| o o | o | o o | o |
|Ted - dy | Bear, | with the | bow, |

| o o | o o | o o | o |
| I love | you from | head to | toe! |

Use with pages 12-13, LESSONS, Primer Level.

Reading
2NDS AND 3RDS

27. NOTE FLASHES: Write the name below the note and then play.

   a. 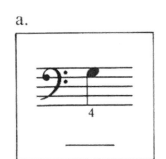   b. 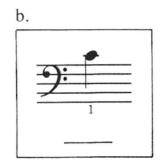   c.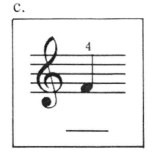

28. INTERVAL FLASHES: Write the names below the two given notes. Identify the interval (2nd or 3rd) and then play.

   a. 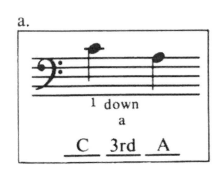   b.    c.

29. READ AND PLAY: Use the following practice directions to play and count aloud the music.
    1. Keep your eyes on the music.
    2. Before playing, clap and count the rhythm aloud.
    3. Prepare the position for both hands on the keyboard - fingers gently curved.
    4. Count aloud as you play slowly.

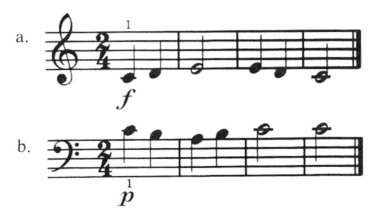

Use with pages 14-15, LESSONS, Primer Level.

Listening
STEPS AND SKIPS, 2NDS AND 3RDS

30. Listen to two notes. The second note will step up or step down from the first note. The first note is shown. Draw the second note.

   a.    b. 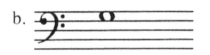   c.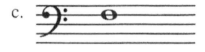

31. Listen to two notes. The second note will skip up or skip down from the first note. The first note is shown. Draw the second note.

   a.    b.    c.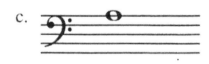

32. Listen to examples in 2/4 or 3/4 time. Circle the correct answer.

   a. 2/4   3/4   b. 2/4   3/4   c. 2/4   3/4

33. Listen to two rhythm patterns. Are they the same or different? Circle the correct answer.

   a. same   b. same   c. same

       different   different   different

34. Listen to intervals of a 2nd or 3rd. Circle the correct answer.

   a. 2nd   b. 2nd   c. 2nd

       3rd   3rd   3rd

Use with page 16, LESSONS, Primer Level.

Reading
2NDS AND 3RDS

35. NOTE FLASHES: Write the name below the note and then play.

a.  b. 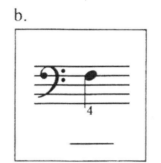 c.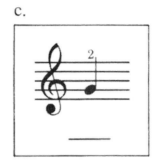

36. INTERVAL FLASHES: Write the names below the two given notes. Identify the interval (2nd or 3rd) and then play.

a. 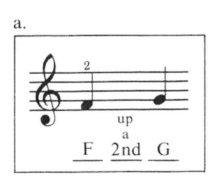 b. 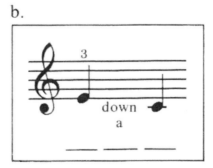 c.

37. READ AND PLAY: Follow the practice directions on page 13 to play and count aloud the music.

Use with pages 17-18, LESSONS, Primer Level.

Listening
QUARTER REST, 2NDS AND 3RDS

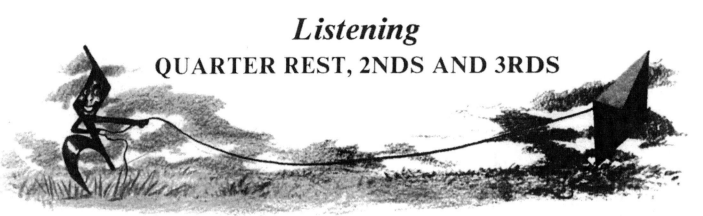

38. Look and listen to the rhythm patterns. Draw the missing note (♩) or rest (𝄽) under the arrow.

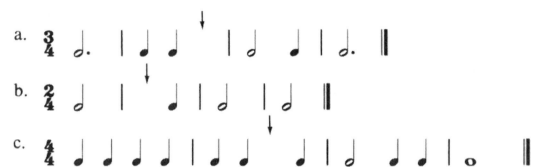

39. Look and listen to four notes. The first three notes are given. Draw the fourth note and then play each pattern.

40. Circle the rhythm pattern that you hear.

41. Look and listen to each rhythm pattern. Add the correct dynamic marking (*f* or *p*) on the line in front of the time signature.

Use with pages 17-18, LESSONS, Primer Level.

Reading
NEW C POSITION

42. **NOTE FLASHES:** Write the name below the note and then play.

   a. 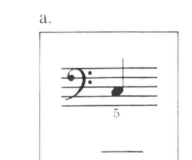   b. 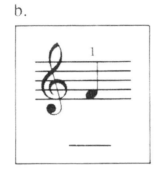   c.

43. **INTERVAL FLASHES:** Write the names below the two given notes. Identify the melodic interval (2nd or 3rd) and the direction (up or down) that it moves. Then play.

   a. 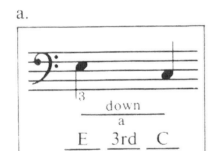   b.    c.

44. **READ AND PLAY:** Follow the practice directions on page 13 to play and count aloud the music.

Use with pages 19-20, LESSONS, Primer Level.

Listening
STEPS AND SKIPS

45. Look and listen to the rhythm pattern. Complete the second measure using ♩ 𝅗𝅥 and 𝅗𝅥. notes.

46. Listen to four notes. The first three notes are given. Draw the fourth note and then play each pattern.

47. Listen to two notes. The second note will step up or step down from E. Draw the second note and write its name below.

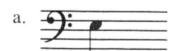   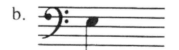   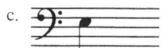

_____   _____   _____

48. Listen to examples in 3/4 or 4/4 time. Circle the correct answer.

a. 3/4   4/4   b. 3/4   4/4   c. 3/4   4/4

Use with page 21, LESSONS, Primer Level.

Listening
LEGATO, 2NDS AND 3RDS

49. Look and listen to two melodies. Draw a slur over the top of the one that is played legato and then play.

50. Listen to two notes. The second note will skip up or skip down from E. Draw the second note and write its name below.

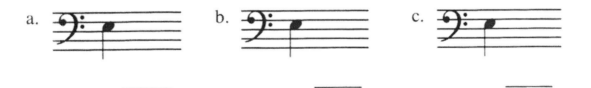

51. Listen to intervals of a 2nd or 3rd. Circle the correct answer.

    a. 2nd   b. 2nd   c. 2nd

         3rd   3rd   3rd

52. Complete the third measure of the piece using any two half notes from the C Position. Play and count aloud.

Use with pages 22-25, LESSONS, Primer Level.

Reading
C POSITION, TIE

53. **NOTE FLASHES:** Write the name below the note and then play.

a. 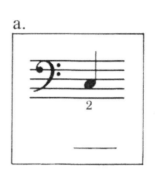 b. 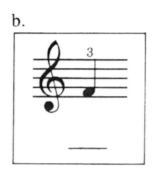 c.

54. **INTERVAL FLASHES:** Write the names below the two given notes. Identify the melodic interval (2nd or 3rd) and the direction (up or down) that it moves. Then play.

a.  b. 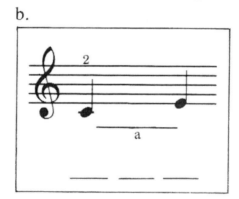 c.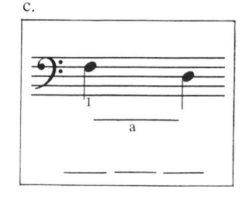

55. **READ AND PLAY:** Follow the practice directions on page 13 to play and count aloud the music.

Use with page 26, LESSONS, Primer Level.

Listening
TIE

56. Look and listen to the rhythm pattern. Add the tie that you hear.

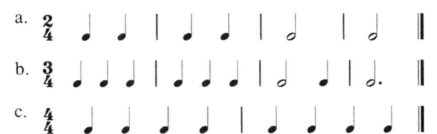

57. Look and listen to the rhythm pattern. Complete the second measure using ♩ ♩ and 𝄽

58. Look and listen to three melodies. Draw the missing note under each arrow.

59. Draw a quarter note a step below the first note of measures one and two. Then play.

Use with page 26, LESSONS, Primer Level.

Listening
MELODIC AND HARMONIC INTERVALS

60. Listen to melodic or harmonic intervals of a 2nd or 3rd. Circle the correct answer.

    a. melodic   b. melodic   c. melodic

       harmonic   harmonic   harmonic

61. Look and listen to two melodies. Draw a slur over the top of the one that is played legato and then play.

62. Complete the second measure of the piece using any three quarter notes from the C Position. Play and count aloud.

Use with pages 27-29, LESSONS, Primer Level.

Reading
INTERVAL OF A 4TH

63. NOTE FLASHES: Write the name below the note and then play.

64. INTERVAL FLASHES: Write the names below the two given notes. Identify the melodic interval (2nd or 4th) and the direction (up or down) that it moves. Then play.

  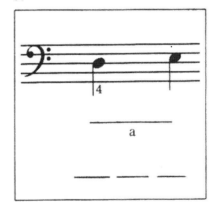

65. READ AND PLAY.

Use with pages 30-31, LESSONS, Primer Level.

Listening
INTERVAL OF A 4TH

66. Listen to melodic or harmonic intervals of a 4th. Circle the correct answer.

   a. melodic   b. melodic   c. melodic

   harmonic   harmonic   harmonic

67. Listen to two notes. The second note will move up a melodic 4th or down a melodic 4th from the first note. The starting key is shown. Write the letter name on the keyboard of the second note that you hear.

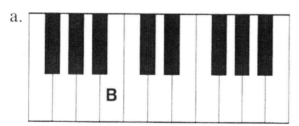 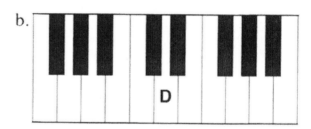

68. Listen to intervals of a 2nd or 4th. Circle the correct answer.

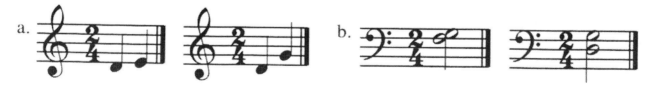

69. Listen to intervals of a 2nd or 4th. Circle the correct answer.

   a. 2nd   b. 2nd   c. 2nd

   4th   4th   4th

Use with page 32, LESSONS, Primer Level.

Reading
INTERVAL OF A 5TH

70. **NOTE FLASHES:** Write the name below the note and then play.

   a. 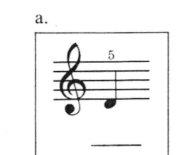 b. 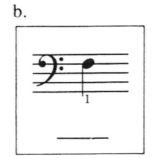 c.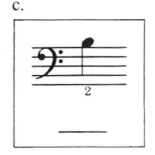

71. **INTERVAL FLASHES:** Write the names below the two given notes. Identify the melodic interval (3rd or 5th) and the direction (up or down) that it moves. Then play.

   a. 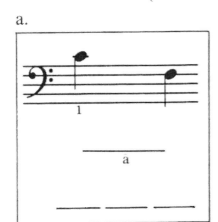 b. 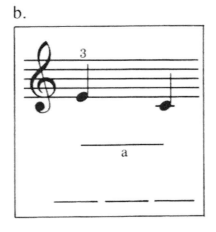 c.

72. **READ AND PLAY.**

Use with pages 33-34, LESSONS, Primer Level.

Listening
INTERVAL OF A 5TH

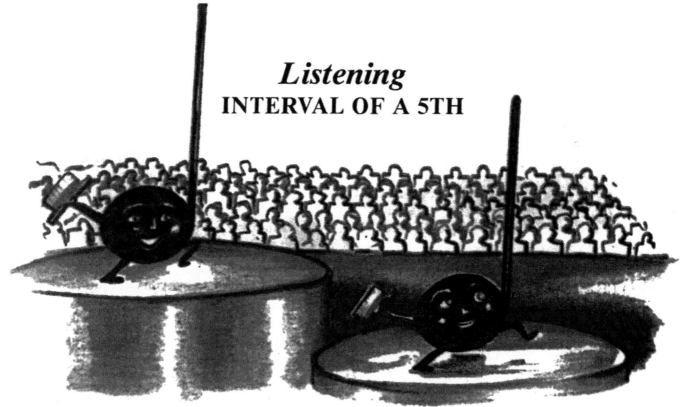

73. Listen to melodic or harmonic intervals of a 5th. Circle the correct answer.

   a. melodic   b. melodic   c. melodic

   harmonic   harmonic   harmonic

74. Listen to two notes. The second note will move up a melodic 5th or down a melodic 5th from the first note. The starting key is shown. Write the letter name on the keyboard of the second note that you hear.

   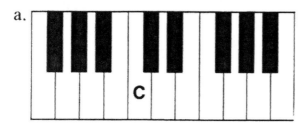 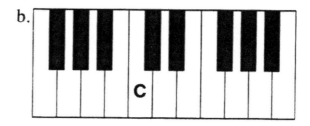

75. Listen to intervals of a 3rd or 5th. Circle the correct answer.

    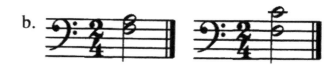

76. Listen to intervals of a 3rd or 5th. Circle the correct answer.

   a. 3rd   b. 3rd   c. 3rd

   5th   5th   5th

Use with pages 33-34, LESSONS, Primer Level.

Listening
FLAT SIGN

77. Listen to two notes. The second note will either repeat or move down (left) to the next key. If the second note moves down, draw a flat sign (♭) in front of it.

78. Listen to intervals of a 4th or 5th. Circle the correct answer.

   a. 4th   b. 4th   c. 4th

       5th   5th   5th

79. Look and listen to the rhythm pattern. Add the tie that you hear.

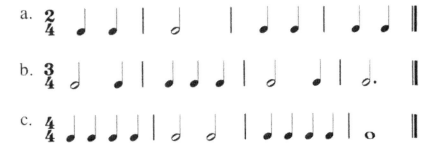

80. Look and listen to three melodies. Draw the missing note under each arrow.

Use with page 35, LESSONS, Primer Level.

Reading
FLAT SIGN

81. NOTE FLASHES: Write the name below the note and then play.

   a. 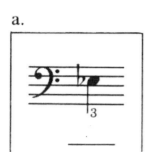   b. 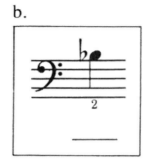   c.

82. INTERVAL FLASHES: Write the names below the two given notes. Identify the melodic interval (4th or 5th) and the direction (up or down) that it moves. Then play.

   a.    b. 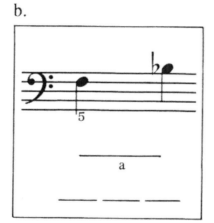   c.

83. READ AND PLAY.

Use with page 36, LESSONS, Primer Level.

Listening
SHARP SIGN

84. Listen to two notes. The second note will either repeat or move up (right) to the next key. If the second note moves up, draw a sharp sign (♯) in front of it.

85. Listen to intervals of a 4th or 5th. Circle the correct answer.

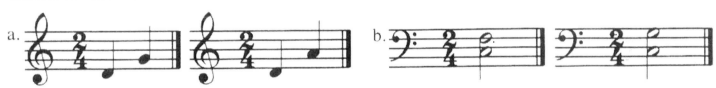

86. Draw a quarter note a melodic 3rd below the first note of measures one and two. Then play.

87. Look and listen to the rhythm pattern. Complete the third measure using ♩ ♩ and 𝄽

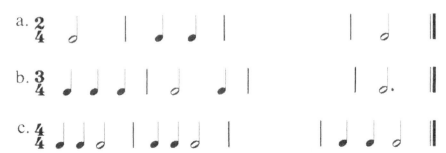

Use with page 37, LESSONS, Primer Level.

Reading
SHARP SIGN

88. **NOTE FLASHES:** Write the name below the note and then play.

89. **INTERVAL FLASHES:** Write the names below the two given notes. Identify the melodic interval (2nd, 3rd, 4th or 5th) and the direction (up or down) that it moves. Then play.

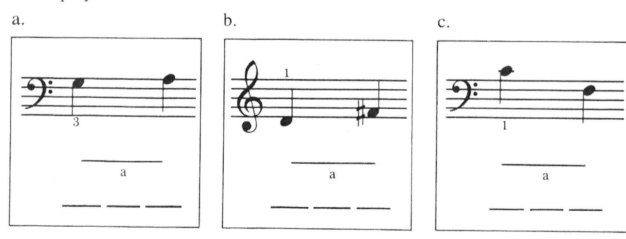

90. **READ AND PLAY.**

Use with page 38, LESSONS, Primer Level.

Reading
G POSITION, STACCATO

READ AND PLAY: Follow the practice directions on page 13 to play and count aloud the music.

91. G Position

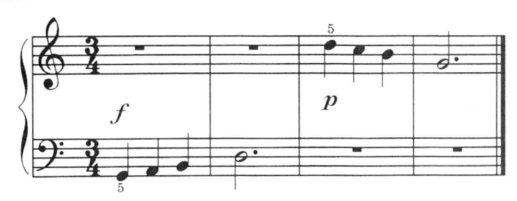

92. Staccato

93. Melodic and Harmonic 2nds and 4ths

a.   b.   c.

94. Melodic and Harmonic 3rd and 5ths

a.   b.   c.

Use with pages 39-40, LESSONS, Primer Level.

Listening
G POSITION, STACCATO

95. Look and listen to two melodies. Add dots under the staccato notes and then play.

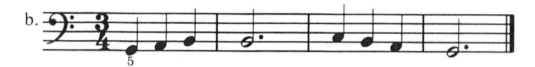

96. Listen to two notes. The second note will move up (right) or down (left) to the next key. If the second note moves up, draw a sharp (♯) sign in front of it. If the second note moves down, draw a flat sign (♭) in front of it.

97. Listen to two notes. The second note will move up a melodic 3rd or 5th from G. Draw the second note and write its name below.

98. Listen to two notes. The second note will move up a melodic 2nd or 4th from G. Draw the second note and write its name below.

Use with pages 41-42, LESSONS, Primer Level.

Reading
REVIEW

99. NOTE FLASHES: Write the name below the note and then play.

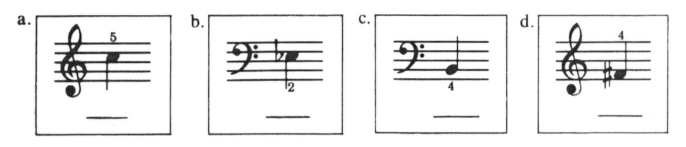

100. INTERVAL FLASHES: Write the names below the two given notes. Identify the melodic interval (2nd, 3rd, 4th or 5th) and the direction (up or down) that it moves. Then play.

Use with page 43, LESSONS, Primer Level.

Listening
REVIEW

101. Look and listen to the rhythm pattern. Complete the second measure using ♩ 𝅗𝅥 𝅗𝅥. and 𝄽

102. Read the words to "Stars" and complete the notes to form the correct rhythm. Use ♩ and 𝅗𝅥.

STARS

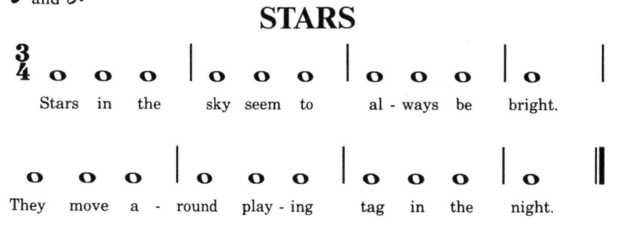

Stars in the sky seem to al - ways be bright.

They move a - round play - ing tag in the night.

103. Complete the second measure of the piece using any two quarter notes from the C position. Play and count aloud.

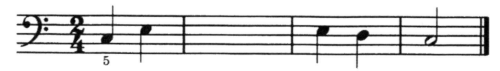

Use with page 43, LESSONS, Primer Level.

Listening REVIEW

Circle the correct answer.

104. The notes are: high   low

105. Which rhythm pattern do you hear?   a   b

     a. $\frac{3}{4}$ ♩ ♩ ♩ | ♩. ‖

     b. $\frac{2}{4}$ ♩ ♩ | ♩ ♩ | ♩ ‖

106. The two rhythm patterns are: same   different

107. The sounds move: up   down

108. The melodic interval is a: step   skip

109. The melody is played: forte (*f*)   piano (*p*)

110. The time signature of this melody is: 2/4   3/4

111. The interval is a: 2nd   3rd

112. The interval is a: 2nd   4th

113. The interval is a: 3rd   5th

114. The interval is a: 4th   5th

115. The melody was played: legato   staccato

Use with pages 44-45, LESSONS, Primer Level.

Listening
REVIEW

116. Look and listen to the rhythm pattern. Add the tie that you hear.

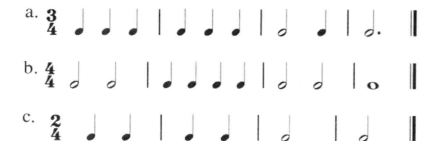

117. Look and listen to three melodies. Draw the missing note under each arrow.

118. Listen to intervals. Write H if it is harmonic or M if it is melodic. Name the interval (3rd or 5th).

a. __H__ __3rd__   b. _____ _____

c. _____ _____   d. _____ _____

Use with page 46, LESSONS, Primer Level.

Reading
REVIEW

READ AND PLAY: Follow the practice directions on page 13 to play and count aloud the music.

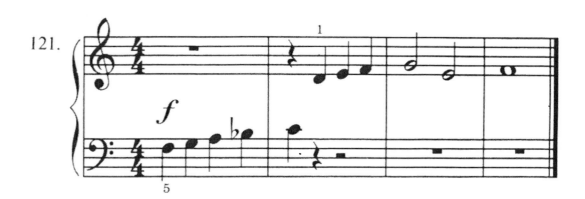

Use with page 46, LESSONS, Primer Level.

Teacher's Pages
SIGHT READING AND EAR TRAINING
Primer Level

Student Book Page | Example Number

4
1. a. high   b. low   c. middle
2. a. higher   b. lower   c. lower
3. a. one   b. more   c. one
4. a. first   b. second   c. first

5
5. (rhythm examples)
6. a. same   b. different   c. different
7. a. down   b. up   c. same
8. a. / b. (rhythm examples)
9. a. / b. / c. (rhythm examples)

6
10. a. Left hand   b. Right hand

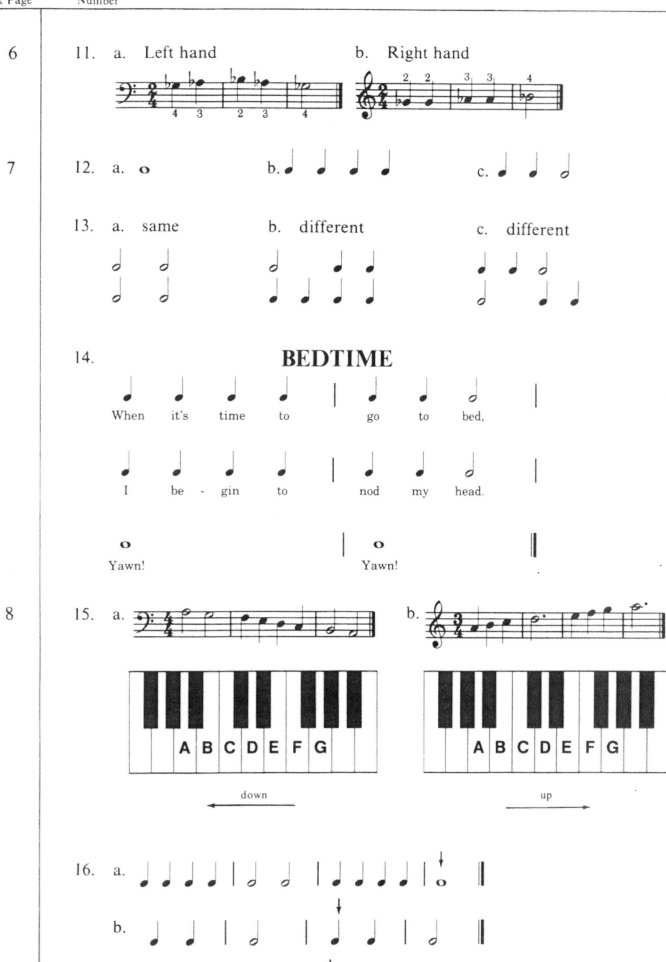

Student Book Page	Example Number		
8	17.	a. 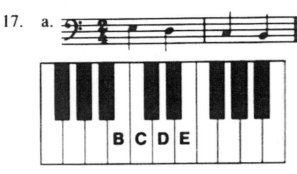	b. 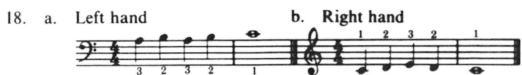
9	18.	a. Left hand b. Right hand  c. Left hand d. Right hand 	
10	19.	a.  c. 	b. 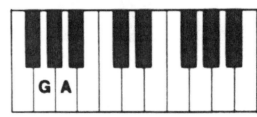 d. 
	20.	a. 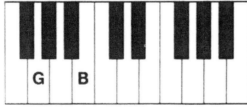 c. 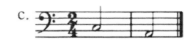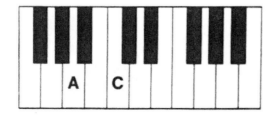	b. 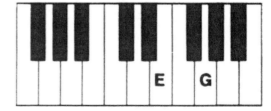 d. 

Student Book Page	Example Number			
11	21.	a. repeat	b. step	c. step
	22.	a. skip	b. skip	c. repeat
	23.	a. step	b. skip	c. step
12	24.	a. 3rd	b. 2nd	c. 2nd
	25.	a. *f*	b. *f*	c. *p*
	26.	**TEDDY BEAR**		

Ted-dy Bear, with the bow,
I love you from head to toe!

13	27.	a. G	b. C	c. F
	28.	a. C down a 3rd A	b. A up a 2nd B	c. E down a 2nd D
	29.	READ AND PLAY: Student plays music.		
14	30.	a. down	b. down	c. up
	31.	a. up	b. down	c. down
	32.	a.	b.	c.

Student Book Page	Example Number			

18 — 47. a. F b. D c. D

48. a. (treble, 4/4) b. (bass, 4/4) c. (treble, 3/4)

19 — 49. a. (bass, 4/4, tied) b. (bass, 4/4, staccato)

50. a. C b. G c. G

51. a. 3rd b. 3rd c. 2nd

52. Student adds two half notes from C position and plays on keyboard.

20 — 53. a. C b. F c. E

54. a. G down a 2nd F   b. C up a 3rd E   c. F down a 3rd D

55. READ AND PLAY: Student plays music.

21 — 56. a. 2/4 b. 3/4 c. 4/4

57. a. 3/4 b. 2/4 c. 4/4

Student Book Page	Example Number	
21	58.	a. 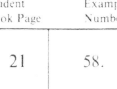
		b.
		c.
	59.	
22	60.	a. harmonic b. harmonic c. melodic
	61.	a.
		b.
	62.	Student adds three quarter notes from C position and plays on keyboard.
23	63.	a. E b. A c. G
	64.	a. A down a 4th E b. D up a 4th G c. D up a 2nd E
	65.	READ AND PLAY: Student plays music.
24	66.	a. melodic b. harmonic c. harmonic
	67.	a. b.
	68.	a. 4th b. 2nd
	69.	a. 4th b. 4th c. 2nd

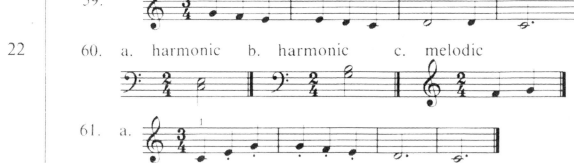

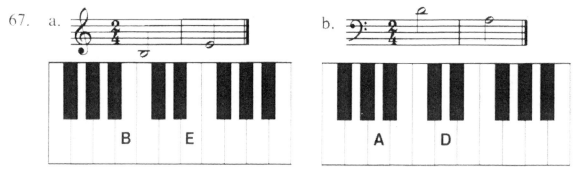

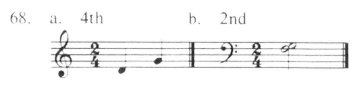

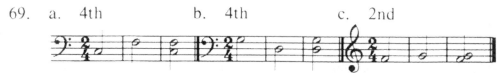

Student Book Page	Example Number			
25	70.	a. D	b. F	c. B
	71.	a. C down a 5th F	b. E down a 3rd C	c. D up a 5th A
	72.	READ AND PLAY: Student plays music.		
26	73.	a. harmonic b. harmonic c. melodic		

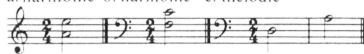

74.

 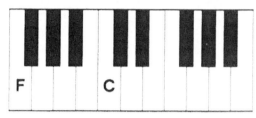

75. a. 3rd   b. 5th

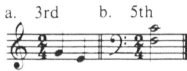

76. a. 5th   b. 3rd   c. 3rd

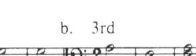

27

77. a.   b.   c.

78. a. 4th   b. 5th   c. 5th

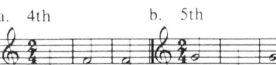

79.

80.

Student Book Page	Example Number			
28	81.	a. E♭	b. B♭	c. A
	82.	a. D up a 5th A	b. F up a 4th B♭	c. G down a 4th D
	83.	READ AND PLAY: Student plays music.		
29	84.	a.	b.	c.

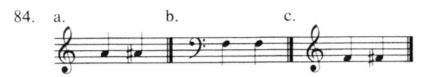

85. a. 5th   b. 4th

86.

87.

a. 2/4 𝅗𝅥 | ♩♩ | 𝄽 | 𝅗𝅥 ‖

b. 3/4 ♩♩♩ | 𝅗𝅥 ♩ | 𝅗𝅥 ♩ | 𝅗𝅥. ‖

c. 4/4 ♩♩𝅗𝅥 | ♩♩♩♩ | ♩♩♩♩ | ♩♩𝅗𝅥 ‖

30	88.	a. A	b. G	c. F♯
	89.	a. G up a 2nd A	b. D up a 3rd F♯	c. C down a 5th F
	90.	READ AND PLAY: Student plays music.		
31	91-94.	READ AND PLAY: Student plays music.		
32	95.	a.		

96. a.   b.   c.

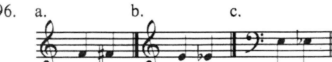

97. a.   b.   c.

B   D   D

98. a.   b.   c.

C   A   C

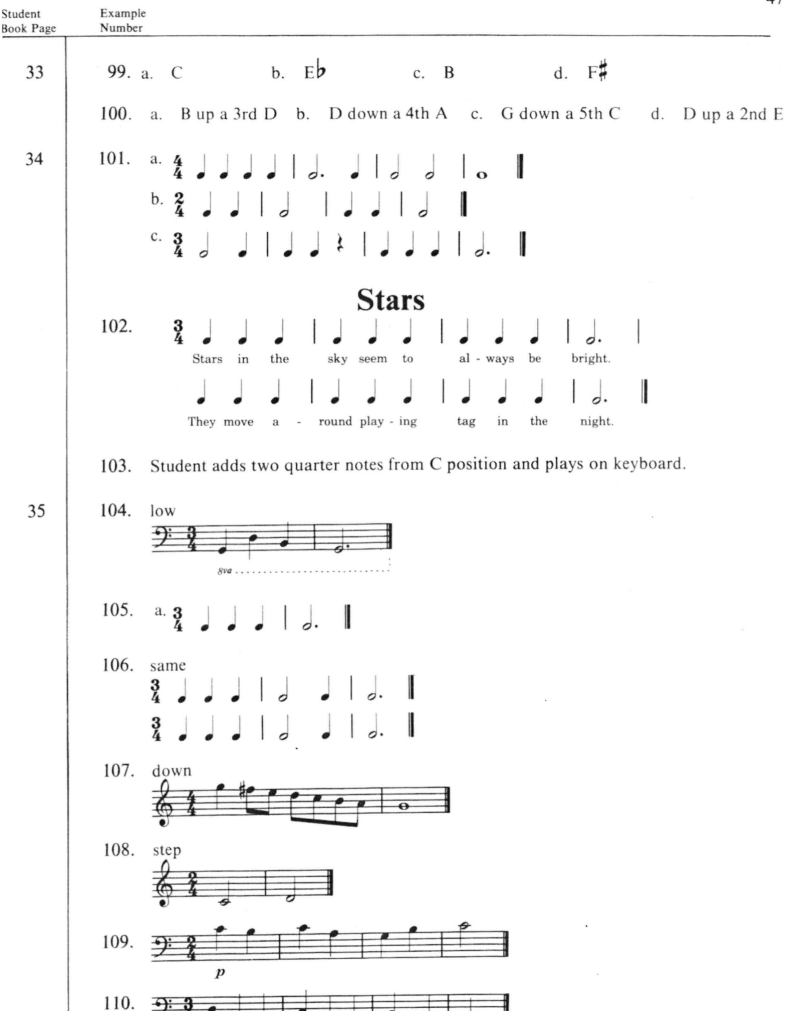

Student Book Page	Example Number	
35	111. 3rd	
	112. 2nd	
	113. 5th	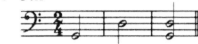
	114. 4th	
	115. legato	
36	116.	
	117.	
	118. a. H 3rd b. M 5th c. H 5th d. M 3rd	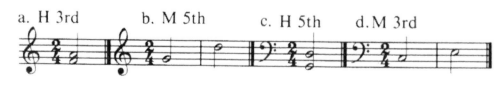
37	119 –122. READ AND PLAY: Student plays music.	